THIS BOOK IS A GIFT TO:

_____

FROM:

_____

DATE:

_____

Visit Christian Art Gifts, Inc. at www.christianartgifts.com.

199 Favorite Bible Verses for Men

© 2008 Christian Art Gifts Inc., IL, USA
Christian Art Publishers, RSA

First edition 2023

Designed by Brad Miedema

Images used under license from Shutterstock.com

ISBN 978-1-63952-235-4

Printed in China

28 27 26 25 24 23
11 10 9 8 7 6 5 4 3 2

101
Favorite
BIBLE VERSES
— FOR MEN —

Christian art gifts®

Contents

What to Do

WHEN I NEED...

- 1 -

Since we have a great priest
over the house of God, let us
draw near to God with a
sincere heart and with the full
assurance that faith brings.

HEBREWS 10:21-22

- 2 -

As far as the east is from the west,
so far has He removed our
transgressions from us.

PSALM 103:12 NKJV

- 3 -

The LORD is my light and my
salvation—whom shall I fear?
The LORD is the stronghold of my
life—of whom shall I be afraid?

PSALM 27:1

- 4 -

"I tell you the truth, those
who listen to My message and
believe in God who sent Me have
eternal life. They will never
be condemned for their sins,
but they have already
passed from death into life."

JOHN 5:24 NLT

- 5 -

"I am the LORD your God
who takes hold of your right
hand and says to you,
'Do not fear; I will help you.'"

ISAIAH 41:13

There's no greater comfort
than to remember that you're
living in the center of God's will—
nothing can ever happen to you
without God's permission.

– ANONYMOUS

BLESSED ASSURANCE,
JESUS IS MINE!
OH, WHAT A FORETASTE
OF GLORY DIVINE!
HEIR OF SALVATION,
PURCHASE OF GOD,
BORN OF HIS SPIRIT,
WASHED IN HIS BLOOD.

– FANNY CROSBY

- 6 -

Being confident of this very thing,
that He who has begun a
good work in you will complete
it until the day of Jesus Christ.

PHILIPPIANS 1:6 NKJV

- 7 -

It is better to take refuge in
the Lord than to trust in princes.

PSALM 118:9 NLT

- 8 -

The Lord will be your
confidence and will keep your
foot from being caught.

PROVERBS 3:26 ESV

Confidence

- 9 -

It is the LORD who goes before
you. He will be with you; He will
not leave you or forsake you.
Do not fear or be dismayed.

DEUTERONOMY 31:8 ESV

- 10 -

So we say with confidence,
"The Lord is my helper; I will
not be afraid. What can
mere mortals do to me?"

HEBREWS 13:6

Expect great things from God;
attempt great things for God.

– WILLIAM CAREY

OH, HOW GREAT
PEACE AND QUIETNESS
WOULD HE POSSESS
WHO SHOULD CUT OFF
ALL VAIN ANXIETY
AND PLACE ALL HIS
CONFIDENCE IN GOD.

– THOMAS À KEMPIS

- 11 -

Do not let your heart faint,
do not be afraid, and do not
tremble or be terrified; for the
LORD your God is He who goes
with you, to fight for you against
your enemies, to save you.

DEUTERONOMY 20:3-4 NKJV

- 12 -

If we are faithful to the end,
trusting God just as firmly as
when we first believed, we will
share in all that belongs to Christ.

HEBREWS 3:14 NLT

- 13 -

God equipped me with
strength and made my way
blameless. He made my feet
like the feet of a deer and set
me secure on the heights.

PSALM 18:32-33 ESV

- 14 -

May our Lord Jesus Christ Himself
and God our Father, who loved us
and by His grace gave us eternal
comfort and a wonderful hope,
comfort you and strengthen you in
every good thing you do and say.

2 THESSALONIANS 2:16-17 NLT

I'll lift you and you lift me,
and we'll both ascend together.

– JOHN GREENLEAF WHITTIER

**ENCOURAGEMENT
COSTS YOU NOTHING
TO GIVE, BUT IS
PRICELESS TO RECEIVE.**

– ANONYMOUS

God's Presence

- 15 -

The LORD replied,
"My Presence will go with you,
and I will give you rest."

EXODUS 33:14

- 16 -

You hide them in the
shelter of Your presence.

PSALM 31:20 NLT

- 17 -

"Even to your old age and gray
hairs I am He, I am He who
will sustain you. I have made you
and I will carry you; I will sustain
you and I will rescue you."

ISAIAH 46:4

- 18 -

"I am with you always,
even to the end of the age."

MATTHEW 28:20 NKJV

- 19 -

"Behold, I stand at the door
and knock. If anyone hears
My voice and opens the door,
I will come in to him and dine
with him, and he with Me."

REVELATION 3:20 NKJV

- 20 -

The LORD is near to all
who call on Him, to all
who call on Him in truth.

PSALM 145:18

Let our chief work as God's messengers
be intercession (prayer); in it we secure the
presence and power of God to go with us.

– ANDREW MURRAY

THE IMPORTANCE
OF COMING INTO
GOD'S PRESENCE IS
WORTH OVERCOMING
ALL OBSTACLES
ALONG THE WAY.

– A.W. TOZER

- 21 -

May the God of hope fill you
with all joy and peace in believing,
that you may abound in hope by
the power of the Holy Spirit.

ROMANS 15:13 NKJV

- 22 -

For You, O Lord, are my hope,
my trust, O LORD, from my youth.

PSALM 71:5 ESV

- 23 -

Let us hold fast the confession
of our hope without wavering,
for He who promised is faithful.

HEBREWS 10:23 NKJV

- 24 -

So be strong and courageous,
all you who put your
hope in the LORD!

PSALM 31:24 NLT

Hope

- 25 -

Those who hope in the LORD
will renew their strength.
They will soar on wings like eagles;
they will run and not grow weary,
they will walk and not be faint.

ISAIAH 40:31

- 26 -

Three things will last forever
—faith, hope, and love.

1 CORINTHIANS 13:13 NLT

Hope is called the anchor of the soul
because it gives stability to the Christian life.
But hope is not simply a "wish"; rather, it is
that which latches on to the certainty of the
promises of the future that God has made.

– R.C. SPROUL

PRAY AS THOUGH
EVERYTHING
DEPENDED ON GOD.
WORK AS THOUGH
EVERYTHING
DEPENDED ON YOU.

– ST. AUGUSTINE

Strength

- 27 -

"My grace is sufficient for you,
for My strength is made
perfect in weakness."

2 CORINTHIANS 12:9 NKJV

- 28 -

He gives power to the faint,
and to him who has no might
He increases strength.

ISAIAH 40:29 ESV

- 29 -

My health may fail, and my
spirit may grow weak,
but God remains the strength
of my heart; He is mine forever.

PSALM 73:26 NLT

Strength

- 30 -

For You equipped me with
strength for the battle;
You made those who rise
against me sink under me.

2 SAMUEL 22:40 ESV

- 31 -

God is my strength and
power, and He makes my way
perfect. He makes my feet like
the feet of deer, and sets
me on my high places.

2 SAMUEL 22:33-34 NKJV

It is the mark of weak men that
they break down under unusual
responsibilities, of strong men
that they are developed by them.

– C. I. SCOFIELD

DO NOT PRAY FOR
EASY LIVES. PRAY TO
BE STRONGER MEN!
DO NOT PRAY FOR TASKS
EQUAL TO YOUR POWERS.
PRAY FOR POWERS
EQUAL TO YOUR TASKS.
THEN THE DOING OF YOUR
WORK SHALL BE NO
MIRACLE, BUT YOU
SHALL BE A MIRACLE.

– PHILLIPS BROOKS

Wisdom

- 32 -

If you need wisdom,
ask our generous God, and
He will give it to you. He will
not rebuke you for asking.

JAMES 1:5 NLT

- 33 -

To the person who pleases Him,
God gives wisdom,
knowledge and happiness.

ECCLESIASTES 2:26

- 34 -

The fear of the LORD is the
beginning of wisdom; a good
understanding have all those
who do His commandments.
His praise endures forever.

PSALM 111:10 NKJV

- 35 -

The wisdom from above is
first pure, then peaceable,
gentle, open to reason, full of
mercy and good fruits, impartial
and sincere. And a harvest of
righteousness is sown in peace
by those who make peace.

JAMES 3:17-18 ESV

- 36 -

Wisdom is sweet to your soul.
If you find it, you will have
a bright future, and your
hopes will not be cut short.

PROVERBS 24:14 NLT

- 37 -

Oh, the depth of the riches of the
wisdom and knowledge of God!
How unsearchable His judgments,
and His paths beyond tracing out!

ROMANS 11:33

HE IS TRULY WISE WHO LOOKS UPON ALL EARTHLY THINGS AS FOLLY THAT HE MAY GAIN CHRIST.

– THOMAS À KEMPIS

What the Bible Says
CONCERNING...

Anger

- 38 -

People with understanding
control their anger; a hot temper
shows great foolishness.

PROVERBS 14:29 NLT

- 39 -

Refrain from anger and turn
from wrath; do not fret—
it leads only to evil.

PSALM 37:8

- 40 -

If possible, so far as it depends
on you, live peaceably with all.

ROMANS 12:18 ESV

- 41 -

"In your anger do not sin":
Do not let the sun go down
while you are still angry.

EPHESIANS 4:26

- 42 -

Don't befriend angry people or
associate with hot-tempered
people, or you will learn to be like
them and endanger your soul.

PROVERBS 22:24-25 NLT

- 43 -

The LORD is compassionate
and gracious, slow to anger,
abounding in love. He does
not treat us as our sins
deserve or repay us
according to our iniquities.

PSALM 103:8, 10

Anger blows out the lamp of the mind.
It's a child's reaction to an adult situation.

– ANONYMOUS

TWO THINGS A MAN
SHOULD NEVER
BE ANGRY AT:
WHAT HE CAN HELP,
AND WHAT HE CANNOT HELP.

– THOMAS FULLER

Discipline

- 44 -

No discipline is enjoyable while
it is happening—it's painful!
But afterward there will
be a peaceful harvest of
right living for those who
are trained in this way.

HEBREWS 12:11 NLT

- 45 -

Blessed is the man whom God
corrects; so do not despise
the discipline of the Almighty.

JOB 5:17

- 46 -

Chasten your son while there
is hope, and do not set your
heart on his destruction.

PROVERBS 19:18 NKJV

Discipline

- 47 -

Discipline your children;
you'll be glad you did—they'll
turn out delightful to live with.

PROVERBS 29:17 The Message

- 48 -

"Think about it: Just as a parent
disciplines a child, the LORD your
God disciplines you for your own
good. So obey the commands
of the LORD your God by walking
in His ways and fearing Him."

DEUTERONOMY 8:5-6 NLT

The goal of God's discipline
is restoration—
never condemnation.

– ANONYMOUS

**DISCIPLINE IS
THE REFINING FIRE
BY WHICH TALENT
BECOMES ABILITY.**

– ROY L. SMITH

- 49 -

See what great love the Father
has lavished on us, that we
should be called children of God!
And that is what we are!

1 JOHN 3:1

- 50 -

"Honor your father and mother.
Then you will live a long,
full life in the land the LORD
your God is giving you."

EXODUS 20:12 NLT

- 51 -

As a father has compassion
on his children, so the
LORD has compassion
on those who fear Him.

PSALM 103:13

Family

- 52 -

"Whoever does the will
of God, he is My brother
and sister and mother."

MARK 3:35 ESV

- 53 -

Train up a child in the way he
should go, and when he is old
he will not depart from it.

PROVERBS 22:6 NKJV

- 54 -

"I will be a Father to you, and you
will be My sons and daughters,
says the Lord Almighty."

2 CORINTHIANS 6:18

The most important thing a
father can do for his children
is to love their mother.

– THEODORE HESBURGH

THE FAMILY WAS ORDAINED
BY GOD BEFORE HE
ESTABLISHED ANY OTHER
INSTITUTION, EVEN BEFORE
HE ESTABLISHED THE CHURCH.

– BILLY GRAHAM

God's Will

- 55 -

Trust in the LORD with all your heart; do not depend on your own understanding. Seek His will in all you do, and He will show you which path to take.

PROVERBS 3:5-6 NLT

- 56 -

Do not be conformed to this world, but be transformed by the renewing of your mind, that you may prove what is that good and acceptable and perfect will of God.

ROMANS 12:2 NKJV

- 57 -

The LORD directs the steps of the godly. He delights in every detail of their lives.

PSALM 37:23 NLT

- 58 -

The LORD says, "I will guide
you along the best pathway
for your life. I will advise
you and watch over you."

PSALM 32:8 NLT

- 59 -

Give thanks in all circumstances;
for this is the will of God in
Christ Jesus for you.

1 THESSALONIANS 5:18 ESV

There is no failure in God's will,
and no success outside of God's will.

– GEORGE W. TREUTT

I FIND THAT DOING
THE WILL OF GOD
LEAVES ME WITH
NO TIME FOR DISPUTING
ABOUT HIS PLANS.

— GEORGE MACDONALD

Humility

- 60 -

Humble yourselves in
the sight of the Lord,
and He will lift you up.

JAMES 4:10 NKJV

- 61 -

"Those who exalt themselves
will be humbled,
and those who humble
themselves will be exalted."

MATTHEW 23:12

- 62 -

Don't be selfish; don't try to
impress others. Be humble,
thinking of others as better than
yourselves. Don't look out only
for your own interests, but take
an interest in others, too.

PHILIPPIANS 2:3-4 NLT

Humility

- 63 -

"Blessed are the meek,
for they will inherit the earth."

MATTHEW 5:5

- 64 -

The reward for humility and
fear of the LORD is riches
and honor and life.

PROVERBS 22:4 ESV

- 65 -

"Whoever takes the lowly position
of this child is the greatest
in the kingdom of heaven."

MATTHEW 18:4

If you plan to build a tall
house of virtues, you must first
lay deep foundations of humility.

– ST. AUGUSTINE

HUMILITY IS NOT AN IDEAL,
IT IS THE UNCONSCIOUS
RESULT OF THE LIFE BEING
RIGHTLY RELATED TO GOD.

– OSWALD CHAMBERS

Integrity

- 66 -

As for me, You uphold me
in my integrity, and set me
before Your face forever.

PSALM 41:12 NKJV

- 67 -

May integrity and honesty protect
me, for I put my hope in You.

PSALM 25:21 NLT

- 68 -

May God Himself, the God of
peace, sanctify you through and
through. May your whole spirit,
soul and body be kept blameless
at the coming of our Lord Jesus
Christ. The one who calls you
is faithful, and He will do it.

1 THESSALONIANS 5:23-24

Integrity

- 69 -

Light shines on the righteous
and joy on the upright in heart.

PSALM 97:11

- 70 -

The Lord God is a sun and shield;
the Lord will give grace and glory;
no good thing will He withhold
from those who walk uprightly.

PSALM 84:11 NKJV

We must be the same person in private
and in public. Only the Christian worldview
gives us the basis for this kind of integrity.

– CHUCK COLSON

INTEGRITY:
THE VIRTUE OF
BEING GOOD WITHOUT
BEING WATCHED.

— ANONYMOUS

Marriage

- 71 -

He who finds a wife finds a
good thing, and obtains
favor from the Lord.

PROVERBS 18:22 NKJV

- 72 -

"A man will leave his
father and mother and
be united to his wife, and
the two will become one flesh."

EPHESIANS 5:31

- 73 -

Husbands, live with your wives in
an understanding way, showing
honor to the woman as the weaker
vessel, since they are heirs with
you of the grace of life, so that
your prayers may not be hindered.

1 PETER 3:7 ESV

- 74 -

May your fountain be blessed,
and may you rejoice in the
wife of your youth.

PROVERBS 5:18

- 75 -

Let the husband render to his wife
the affection due her, and likewise
also the wife to her husband.

1 CORINTHIANS 7:3 NKJV

Let the wife make the husband
glad to come home, and let him
make her sorry to see him leave.

– MARTIN LUTHER

THE MAN WHO SANCTIFIES
HIS WIFE UNDERSTANDS
THAT THIS IS HIS DIVINELY
ORDAINED RESPONSIBILITY...
IS MY WIFE MORE LIKE
CHRIST BECAUSE SHE IS
MARRIED TO ME? OR IS SHE
LIKE CHRIST IN SPITE OF ME?
HAS SHE SHRUNK FROM HIS
LIKENESS BECAUSE OF ME?
DO I SANCTIFY HER OR
HOLD HER BACK? IS SHE A
BETTER WOMAN BECAUSE
SHE IS MARRIED TO ME?

— R. KENT HUGHES

Priorities

- 76 -

"No one can serve two masters.
Either you will hate the one and
love the other, or you will be
devoted to the one and despise
the other. You cannot serve
both God and money."

MATTHEW 6:24

- 77 -

"Seek the Kingdom of God
above all else, and live
righteously, and He will give
you everything you need."

MATTHEW 6:33 NLT

- 78 -

"Where your treasure is,
there your heart will be also."

MATTHEW 6:21

Priorities

- 79 -

"If anyone would come after
Me, let him deny himself and take
up his cross and follow Me.
For whoever would save his life
will lose it, but whoever loses his
life for My sake will find it.
For what will it profit a man if
he gains the whole world and
forfeits his life? Or what shall a
man give in return for his life?"

MATTHEW 16:24-26 ESV

Lord, we don't mind who is
second as long as Thou art first.

– W. E. SANGSTER

YOU CAN'T GET SECOND
THINGS BY PUTTING
THEM FIRST; YOU CAN
GET SECOND THINGS
ONLY BY PUTTING
FIRST THINGS FIRST.

– C. S. LEWIS

Wealth

- 80 -

It is a good thing to receive wealth
from God and the good health
to enjoy it. To enjoy your work
and accept your lot in life—
that is indeed a gift from God.

ECCLESIASTES 5:19 NLT

- 81 -

"Seek first the kingdom of
God and His righteousness,
and all these things
shall be added to you."

MATTHEW 6:33 NKJV

- 82 -

I have learned how to be
content with whatever I have.
I have learned the secret of
living in every situation.

PHILIPPIANS 4:11-12 NLT

Wealth

- 83 -

Keep your life free
from love of money,
and be content with
what you have.

HEBREWS 13:5 ESV

- 84 -

Those who trust in their riches
will fall, but the righteous
will thrive like a green leaf.

PROVERBS 11:28

If you want to feel rich, just count all the
things you have that money can't buy.

– ANONYMOUS

IT DOES NOT SPOIL
YOUR HAPPINESS TO
CONFESS YOUR SIN.
THE UNHAPPINESS
IS IN NOT MAKING
THE CONFESSION.

– CHARLES SPURGEON

Rely on
God for...

- 85 -

Many are the plans in the mind
of a man, but it is the purpose
of the LORD that will stand.

PROVERBS 19:21 ESV

- 86 -

"For I know the plans I have
for you," declares the LORD,
"plans to prosper you and not
to harm you, plans to give
you hope and a future."

JEREMIAH 29:11

- 87 -

The LORD will fulfill His purpose for
me; Your steadfast love, O LORD,
endures forever. Do not forsake
the work of Your hands.

PSALM 138:8 ESV

- 88 -

Consider the blameless,
observe the upright; a future
awaits those who seek peace.

PSALM 37:37

- 89 -

Don't brag about tomorrow,
since you don't know what
the day will bring.

PROVERBS 27:1 NLT

We must meet the uncertainties
of this world with the
certainty of the world to come.

– A.W. TOZER

LEAVE THE BROKEN, IRREVERSIBLE PAST IN GOD'S HANDS, AND STEP OUT INTO THE INVINCIBLE FUTURE WITH HIM.

– OSWALD CHAMBERS

- 90 -

This God is our God for ever
and ever; He will be our
guide even to the end.

PSALM 48:14

- 91 -

A man's heart plans his way,
but the LORD directs his steps.

PROVERBS 16:9 NKJV

- 92 -

He will not let your foot slip—
He who watches over you will
not slumber; indeed, He who
watches over Israel will neither
slumber nor sleep. The LORD
watches over you—the LORD is
your shade at your right hand;
the sun will not harm you by day,
nor the moon by night.

PSALM 121:3-6

Guidance

- 93 -

The LORD says, "I will guide
you along the best pathway
for your life. I will advise you
and watch over you."

PSALM 32:8 NLT

- 94 -

The steps of a man are
established by the LORD,
when He delights in his way.

PSALM 37:23 ESV

- 95 -

Show me Your ways, O LORD;
teach me Your paths. Lead me
in Your truth and teach me, for
You are the God of my salvation;
on You I wait all the day.

PSALM 25:4-5 NKJV

I AM SATISFIED THAT
WHEN THE ALMIGHTY
WANTS ME TO DO
OR NOT TO DO ANY
PARTICULAR THING,
HE FINDS A WAY OF
LETTING ME KNOW.

– ABRAHAM LINCOLN

Help

- 96 -

I will lift up my eyes to the hills—
from whence comes my help?
My help comes from the LORD,
who made heaven and earth.

PSALM 121:1-2 NKJV

- 97 -

God is our refuge and strength,
an ever-present help in trouble.

PSALM 46:1

- 98 -

The LORD is my strength and my
shield; in Him my heart trusts, and
I am helped; my heart exults, and
with my song I give thanks to Him.

PSALM 28:7 ESV

- 99 -

The LORD is good, a stronghold
in the day of trouble; and He
knows those who trust in Him.

NAHUM 1:7 NKJV

GOD, WHO FORESAW
YOUR TRIBULATION,
HAS SPECIALLY ARMED
YOU TO GO THROUGH IT,
NOT WITHOUT PAIN
BUT WITHOUT STAIN.

– C. S. LEWIS

Patience

- 100 -

Wait for the LORD; be strong and take heart and wait for the LORD.

PSALM 27:14

- 101 -

You also be patient. Establish your hearts, for the coming of the Lord is at hand.

JAMES 5:8 NKJV

- 102 -

The Lord isn't really being slow about His promise, as some people think. No, He is being patient for your sake. He does not want anyone to be destroyed, but wants everyone to repent.

2 PETER 3:9 NLT

Patience

- 103 -

I waited patiently for the LORD; He
inclined to me and heard my cry.

PSALM 40:1 ESV

- 104 -

Since God chose you to be
the holy people He loves, you
must clothe yourselves with
tenderhearted mercy,
kindness, humility,
gentleness, and patience.

COLOSSIANS 3:12 NLT

Patience with others is love.
Patience with self is hope.
Patience with God is faith.

– ADEL BESTAVROS

**PATIENCE IS THE ABILITY
TO SUFFER A LONG TIME
UNDER THE MISTREATMENT OF
OTHERS WITHOUT GROWING
RESENTFUL OR BITTER.**

— JERRY BRIDGES

Peace of Mind

- 105 -

"I am leaving you with a gift—
peace of mind and heart.
And the peace I give is a
gift the world cannot give.
So don't be troubled or afraid."

JOHN 14:27 NLT

- 106 -

I will both lie down in peace,
and sleep; for You alone, O LORD,
make me dwell in safety.

PSALM 4:8 NKJV

- 107 -

You will keep in perfect peace
all who trust in You, all whose
thoughts are fixed on You!

ISAIAH 26:3 NLT

- 108 -

May the Lord of peace Himself
give you His peace at all
times and in every situation.
The Lord be with you all.

2 THESSALONIANS 3:16 NLT

- 109 -

Let the peace of Christ rule in your
hearts, since as members of one
body you were called to peace.
And be thankful.

COLOSSIANS 3:15

Peace is the deliberate adjustment
of my life to the will of God.

– ANONYMOUS

AS WE POUR OUT
OUR BITTERNESS,
GOD POURS IN HIS PEACE.

— F.B. MEYER

- 110 -

"Your Father knows the
things you have need of
before you ask Him."

MATTHEW 6:8 NKJV

- 111 -

My God will meet all your needs
according to the riches of
His glory in Christ Jesus.

PHILIPPIANS 4:19

- 112 -

His divine power has granted to
us all things that pertain to life and
godliness, through the knowledge
of Him who called us to His own
glory and excellence, by which
He has granted to us His precious
and very great promises.

2 PETER 1:3-4 ESV

- 113 -

Don't forget to do good and to
share with those in need. These
are the sacrifices that please God.

HEBREWS 13:16 NLT

- 114 -

"He will give grass in your
fields for your livestock,
and you shall eat and be full."

DEUTERONOMY 11:15 ESV

To believe that He will preserve us is,
indeed, a means of preservation.

– JOHN OWEN

IF GOD SENDS US
ON STONY PATHS,
HE WILL PROVIDE US
WITH STRONG SHOES.

— ALEXANDER MACLAREN

Success

- 115 -

Commit to the LORD whatever you do,
and He will establish your plans.

PROVERBS 16:3

- 116 -

I know the thoughts I think
toward you, says the LORD,
thoughts of peace and
not of evil, to give you a
future and a hope.

JEREMIAH 29:11 NKJV

- 117 -

Whatever you do, work at it
with all your heart, as working
for the Lord, not for human
masters, since you know that
you will receive an inheritance
from the Lord as a reward.

COLOSSIANS 3:23-24

-118 -

It is not that we think we
are qualified to do
anything on our own.
Our qualification comes from God.

2 CORINTHIANS 3:5 NLT

- 119 -

May the LORD give you the
desire of your heart and
make all your plans succeed.

PSALM 20:4

The key to happiness is having
dreams. The key to success is
making your dreams come true.

– ANONYMOUS

God Freely
Gives...

Comfort

- 120 -

Praise be to the God and Father
of our Lord Jesus Christ,
the Father of compassion and
the God of all comfort, who
comforts us in all our troubles.

2 CORINTHIANS 1:3-4

- 121 -

"Blessed are those who mourn,
for they shall be comforted."

MATTHEW 5:4 NKJV

- 122 -

"As a mother comforts her
child, so will I comfort you;
and you will be comforted."

ISAIAH 66:13

- 123 -

"I will not leave you comfortless:
I will come to you."

JOHN 14:18 KJV

- 124 -

Cast your burden on the LORD,
and He shall sustain you;
He shall never permit the
righteous to be moved.

PSALM 55:22 NKJV

God often comforts us, not by changing
the circumstances of our lives, but by
changing our attitude toward them.

– S. H. B. MASTERMAN

GOD DOES NOT COMFORT US TO MAKE US COMFORTABLE, BUT TO MAKE US COMFORTERS.

— J. H. JOWETT

Courage

- 125 -

Be of good courage, and He
shall strengthen your heart,
all you who hope in the LORD.

PSALM 31:24 NKJV

- 126 -

"Be strong and courageous.
Do not be frightened, and do
not be dismayed, for the LORD your
God is with you wherever you go."

JOSHUA 1:9 ESV

- 127 -

In Your strength I can
crush an army; with my
God I can scale any wall.

PSALM 18:29 NLT

Courage

- 128 -

"Fear not, for I am with you; be
not dismayed, for I am your God;
I will strengthen you, I will help
you, I will uphold you with
My righteous right hand."

ISAIAH 41:10 ESV

- 129 -

Having hope will give you
courage. You will be protected
and will rest in safety.

JOB 11:18 NLT

Courage is contagious.
When a brave man takes a stand,
the spines of others are often stiffened.

– BILLY GRAHAM

THE PARADOX OF COURAGE
IS THAT A MAN MUST BE A
LITTLE CARELESS OF HIS LIFE
EVEN IN ORDER TO KEEP IT.

— G.K. CHESTERTON

Forgiveness

- 130 -

If we confess our sins, He is
faithful and just to forgive us
our sins and to cleanse us
from all unrighteousness.

1 JOHN 1:9 ESV

- 131 -

"I will forgive their wickedness,
and I will never again
remember their sins."

HEBREWS 8:12 NLT

- 132 -

"Come now, let us settle
the matter," says the LORD.
"Though your sins are like scarlet,
they shall be as white as snow;
though they are red as crimson,
they shall be like wool."

ISAIAH 1:18

- 133 -

"If My people who are called by
My name will humble themselves,
and pray and seek My face, and
turn from their wicked ways,
then I will hear from heaven,
and will forgive their
sin and heal their land."

2 CHRONICLES 7:14 NKJV

- 134 -

"When you stand praying,
if you hold anything against
anyone, forgive them,
so that your Father in heaven
may forgive you your sins."

MARK 11:25

We win by tenderness;
we conquer by forgiveness.

– FREDERICK W. ROBERTSON

WE HAVE A FREE, FULL, FINAL, FOREVER FORGIVENESS IN THE ATONING WORK OF CHRIST.

– J. SIDLOW BAXTER

Grace

- 135 -

"My grace is all you need.
My power works best in weakness."

2 CORINTHIANS 12:9 NLT

- 136 -

Where sin increased,
grace increased all the more.

ROMANS 5:20

- 137 -

God is able to make all grace
abound toward you, that you,
always having all sufficiency
in all things, may have an
abundance for every good work.

2 CORINTHIANS 9:8 NKJV

Grace

- 138 -

"God opposes the proud but gives grace to the humble."

JAMES 4:6 ESV

- 139 -

You know the grace of our Lord Jesus Christ, that though He was rich, yet for your sake He became poor, so that you through His poverty might become rich.

2 CORINTHIANS 8:9

Grace is but glory begun,
and glory is but grace perfected.

– JONATHAN EDWARDS

THE WORD GRACE
IS UNQUESTIONABLY
THE MOST SIGNIFICANT
SINGLE WORD IN THE BIBLE.

– ILION T. JONES

Love

- 140 -

For God so loved the world that
He gave His one and only Son,
that whoever believes in Him shall
not perish but have eternal life.

JOHN 3:16

- 141 -

Show deep love for each other,
for love covers a multitude of sins.

1 PETER 4:8 NLT

- 142 -

Love is patient, love is kind. It does
not envy, it does not boast, it is not
proud. It does not dishonor others,
it is not self-seeking, it is not easily
angered, it keeps no record of
wrongs. Love does not delight in evil
but rejoices with the truth. It always
protects, always trusts, always hopes,
always perseveres. Love never fails.

1 CORINTHIANS 13:4-8

- 143 -

"A new command I give you:
Love one another. As I have
loved you, so you must love
one another. By this everyone
will know that you are My
disciples, if you love one another."

JOHN 13:34-35

- 144 -

I am persuaded that neither
death nor life, nor angels nor
principalities nor powers, nor
things present nor things to come,
nor height nor depth, nor any
other created thing, shall
be able to separate us from
the love of God which is in
Christ Jesus our Lord.

ROMANS 8:38-39 NKJV

**HUMAN LOVE FAILS
AND WILL ALWAYS FAIL.
GOD'S LOVE NEVER FAILS.**

– CORRIE TEN BOOM

- 145 -

The LORD is gracious and full
of compassion, slow to anger
and great in mercy. The LORD
is good to all, and His tender
mercies are over all His works.

PSALM 145:8-9 NKJV

- 146 -

Because of God's tender mercy,
the morning light from heaven is
about to break upon us, to give
light to those who sit in darkness
and in the shadow of death, and
to guide us to the path of peace.

LUKE 1:78-79 NLT

- 147 -

To the Lord our God belong
mercy and forgiveness.

DANIEL 9:9 ESV

- 148 -

God saved us, not because of
the righteous things we had done,
but because of His mercy.

TITUS 3:5 NLT

- 149 -

"Blessed are the merciful,
for they will be shown mercy.
Blessed are the pure in heart,
for they will see God."

MATTHEW 5:7-8

Two words of mercy set a man free:
forgive and you will be forgiven,
and give and you will receive.

– ST. AUGUSTINE

TEACH ME TO FEEL
ANOTHER'S WOE,
TO HIDE THE FAULT I SEE;
THAT MERCY I TO OTHERS
SHOW, THAT MERCY
SHOW TO ME.

– ALEXANDER POPE

Self-Control

- 150 -

Guard your heart above
all else, for it determines
the course of your life.

PROVERBS 4:23 NLT

- 151 -

God gave us a spirit not
of fear but of power and
love and self-control.

2 TIMOTHY 1:7 ESV

- 152 -

So prepare your minds for
action and exercise self-control.
Put all your hope in the gracious
salvation that will come to you
when Jesus Christ is revealed to
the world. So you must live as
God's obedient children. Don't
slip back into your old ways of
living to satisfy your own desires.

1 PETER 1:13-14 NLT

Self-Control

- 153 -

Make every effort to add to your
faith goodness; and to goodness,
knowledge; and to knowledge,
self-control; and to self-control,
perseverance; and to perseverance,
godliness; and to godliness, mutual
affection; and to mutual affection,
love. For if you possess these
qualities in increasing measure,
they will keep you from being
ineffective and unproductive in your
knowledge of our Lord Jesus Christ.

2 PETER 1:5-8

No conflict is so severe as his
who labors to subdue himself.

– THOMAS À KEMPIS

**TRUE SELF-CONTROL
IS NOT ABOUT BRINGING
OURSELVES UNDER OUR
OWN CONTROL BUT UNDER
THE POWER OF CHRIST.**

– DAVID MATHIS

God Wants

YOU TO...

Be Bold

- 154 -

So we may boldly say:
"The LORD is my helper; I will not
fear. What can man do to me?"

HEBREWS 13:6 NKJV

- 155 -

Wait for the LORD; be strong,
and let your heart take
courage; wait for the LORD!

PSALM 27:14 ESV

- 156 -

"Be strong and courageous.
Do not be terrified; do not
be discouraged, for the
LORD your God will be
with you wherever you go."

JOSHUA 1:9

Be Bold

- 157 -

"Fear not, for I am with you;
be not dismayed, for I am your
God. I will strengthen you, yes,
I will help you, I will uphold you
with My righteous right hand."

ISAIAH 41:10 NKJV

- 158 -

Overwhelming victory is ours
through Christ, who loved us.

ROMANS 8:37 NLT

I am only one, but still I am one.
I cannot do everything,
but still I can do something;
I will not refuse to do the
something I can do.

– HELEN KELLER

IT IS BETTER TO MAKE
A THOUSAND FAILURES
THAN TO BE TOO
COWARDLY TO EVER
UNDERTAKE ANYTHING.

– CLOVIS G. CHAPPELL

Be Kind

- 159 -

But the Holy Spirit produces
this kind of fruit in our lives:
love, joy, peace, patience,
kindness, goodness, faithfulness,
gentleness, and self-control.

GALATIANS 5:22-23 NLT

- 160 -

Instead be kind to each other,
tenderhearted, forgiving
one another, as God through
Christ has forgiven you.

EPHESIANS 4:32 NLT

- 161 -

Your kindness will reward you,
but your cruelty will destroy you.

PROVERBS 11:17 NLT

Be Kind

- 162 -

Make sure that nobody
pays back wrong for wrong,
but always strive to do what
is good for each other
and for everyone else.

1 THESSALONIANS 5:15

- 163 -

Whoever is kind to the
needy honors God.

PROVERBS 14:31

The person who sows seeds of
kindness enjoys a perpetual harvest.

– ANONYMOUS

I CHOOSE KINDNESS...
I WILL BE KIND TO THE POOR,
FOR THEY ARE ALONE.
KIND TO THE RICH, FOR
THEY ARE AFRAID. AND KIND
TO THE UNKIND, FOR SUCH
IS HOW GOD HAS TREATED ME.

– MAX LUCADO

Be a Leader

- 164 -

"Whoever wants to become great among you must be your servant, and whoever wants to be first must be slave of all. For even the Son of Man did not come to be served, but to serve, and to give His life as a ransom for many."

MARK 10:43-45

- 165 -

Let no one despise you for your youth, but set the believers an example in speech, in conduct, in love, in faith, in purity. Persist in this, for by so doing you will save both yourself and your hearers.

1 TIMOTHY 4:12, 16 ESV

- 166 -

Work hard and become a leader.

PROVERBS 12:24 NLT

Be a Leader

- 167 -

He must manage his own
family well and see that
his children obey him.

1 TIMOTHY 3:4

- 168 -

He has told you, O man, what is
good; and what does the Lord
require of you but to do justice,
and to love kindness, and to
walk humbly with your God?

MICAH 6:8 ESV

- 169 -

A good leader motivates,
doesn't mislead, doesn't
exploit. God cares about
honesty in the workplace;
your business is His business.

PROVERBS 16:10-11 THE MESSAGE

**LEADERS WHO
DEVELOP PEOPLE, ADD.
LEADERS WHO DEVELOP
LEADERS, MULTIPLY.**

– JOHN C. MAXWELL

Be Modest

- 170 -

Do not be rash with your mouth,
and let not your heart utter
anything hastily before God.
For God is in heaven,
and you on earth; therefore
let your words be few.

ECCLESIASTES 5:2 NKJV

- 171 -

Don't call attention to yourself;
let others do that for you.

PROVERBS 27:2 THE MESSAGE

- 172 -

God gives us more grace.
That is why Scripture says:
"God opposes the proud but
shows favor to the humble."

JAMES 4:6

Be Modest

- 173 -

Do not boast about tomorrow,
for you do not know
what a day may bring.

PROVERBS 27:1 ESV

- 174 -

Pride ends in humiliation,
while humility brings honor.

PROVERBS 29:23 NLT

It was pride that changed angels into devils;
it is humility that makes men as angels.

– ST. AUGUSTINE

THE HOLY SPIRIT FINDS
MODESTY SO RARE THAT
HE TAKES CARE TO RECORD IT.
SAY MUCH OF WHAT THE
LORD HAS DONE FOR YOU,
BUT SAY LITTLE OF WHAT YOU
HAVE DONE FOR THE LORD.
DO NOT UTTER A SELF-
GLORIFYING SENTENCE!

– CHARLES H. SPURGEON

Pray

- 175 -

The earnest prayer of a righteous
person has great power and
produces wonderful results.

JAMES 5:16 NLT

- 176 -

The LORD is near to all who call
on Him, to all who call on Him
in truth. He fulfills the desires
of those who fear Him; He hears
their cry and saves them.

PSALM 145:18-19

- 177 -

"Whatever you ask in prayer,
you will receive, if you have faith."

MATTHEW 21:22 ESV

Pray

- 178 -

"But when you pray, go into your
room, close the door and pray
to your Father, who is unseen.
Then your Father, who sees what
is done in secret, will reward you."

MATTHEW 6:6

- 179 -

"I say to you, whatever things
you ask when you pray,
believe that you receive them,
and you will have them."

MARK 11:24 NKJV

Prayer should not be regarded as a duty
which must be performed, but rather as
a privilege to be enjoyed, a rare delight
that is always revealing some new beauty.

– E. M. BOUNDS

THE MEN WHO HAVE DONE
THE MOST FOR GOD IN
THIS WORLD HAVE BEEN
EARLY ON THEIR KNEES.

– E. M. BOUNDS

- 180 -

Blessed is the man who endures
temptation; for when he has been
approved, he will receive the
crown of life which the Lord has
promised to those who love Him.

JAMES 1:12 NKJV

- 181 -

Therefore, my beloved brothers,
be steadfast, immovable, always
abounding in the work of the
Lord, knowing that in the Lord
your labor is not in vain.

1 CORINTHIANS 15:58 ESV

- 182 -

"The one who endures
to the end will be saved."

MATTHEW 24:13 NLT

- 183 -

Not only so, but we also glory in our sufferings, because we know that suffering produces perseverance; perseverance, character; and character, hope. And hope does not put us to shame, because God's love has been poured out into our hearts through the Holy Spirit, who has been given to us.

ROMANS 5:3-5

- 184 -

"Because you have obeyed My command to persevere, I will protect you from the great time of testing that will come upon the whole world to test those who belong to this world."

REVELATION 3:10 NLT

By perseverance the snail reached the ark.

– CHARLES H. SPURGEON

OUR MOTTO MUST CONTINUE
TO BE PERSEVERANCE.
AND ULTIMATELY I TRUST
THE ALMIGHTY WILL CROWN
OUR EFFORTS WITH SUCCESS.

– WILLIAM WILBERFORCE

Respect Others

- 185 -

Do nothing out of selfish
ambition or vain conceit.
Rather in humility value
others above yourselves.

PHILIPPIANS 2:3

- 186 -

You, dear friends, must
build each other up in your
most holy faith, pray in the
power of the Holy Spirit.

JUDE 20 NLT

- 187 -

"Honor your father and
your mother, so that you may
live long in the land the
LORD your God is giving you."

EXODUS 20:12

Respect Others

- 188 -

Pay to all what is owed to them:
taxes to whom taxes are owed,
revenue to whom revenue
is owed, respect to whom
respect is owed, honor
to whom honor is owed.

ROMANS 13:7 ESV

- 189 -

Show proper respect to everyone,
love the family of believers.

1 PETER 2:17

He that respects not is not respected.

– GEORGE HERBERT

ALL OF US WOULD BE
WISER IF WE WOULD
RESOLVE NEVER TO
PUT PEOPLE DOWN,
EXCEPT ON OUR
PRAYER LISTS.

– D.A. CARSON

Work

- 190 -

Whatever you do, work at it with
all your heart, as working for the
Lord, not for human masters,
since you know that you will
receive an inheritance from
the Lord as a reward. It is the
Lord Christ you are serving.

COLOSSIANS 3:23-24

- 191 -

His lord said to him, "Well done,
good and faithful servant;
you have been faithful over
a few things, I will make
you ruler over many things.
Enter into the joy of your lord."

MATTHEW 25:23 NKJV

- 192 -

Do your best to present yourself
to God as one approved, a worker
who has no need to be ashamed,
rightly handling the word of truth.

2 TIMOTHY 2:15 ESV

- 193 -

The LORD will open the heavens,
the storehouse of His bounty, to send
rain on your land in season and
to bless all the work of your hands.

DEUTERONOMY 28:12

- 194 -

"Take My yoke upon you, and
learn from Me, for I am gentle and
lowly in heart, and you will find
rest for your souls. For My yoke
is easy, and My burden is light."

MATTHEW 11:29-30 ESV

If our identity is in our work, rather
than Christ, success will go to our heads,
and failure will go to our hearts.

– TIM KELLER

YOUR ATTITUDE,
NOT YOUR APTITUDE,
DETERMINES
YOUR ALTITUDE.

— ZIG ZIGLAR

Worship

- 195 -

"God is spirit, and His
worshipers must worship
in the Spirit and in truth."

JOHN 4:24

- 196 -

Honor the LORD for the glory of
His name. Worship the LORD in
the splendor of His holiness.

PSALM 29:2 NLT

- 197 -

So here's what I want you to do,
God helping you: Take your
everyday, ordinary life—your
sleeping, eating, going-to-work,
and walking-around life—and
place it before God as an offering.
Embracing what God does
for you is the best thing
you can do for Him.

ROMANS 12:1 THE MESSAGE

Worship

- 198 -

I praise You because I am
fearfully and wonderfully made;
Your works are wonderful,
I know that full well.

PSALM 139:14

- 199 -

For great is the LORD, and greatly
to be praised, and He is to
be feared above all gods.

1 CHRONICLES 16:25 ESV

The more a man bows his knee before God,
the straighter he stands before men.

– ANONYMOUS

IT IS ONLY WHEN MEN
BEGIN TO WORSHIP
THAT THEY BEGIN TO GROW.

– CALVIN COOLIDGE

Notes